Tricky Brain Puzzles

With illustrations by
Tamar de Wit

Musclemen

Which gorilla is lifting the heaviest weights?

$14 \times 4 - 4$

$9 \times 4 + 12$

$26 \times 2 - 4$

$24 \times 2 + 4$

Danny

Billy

Dinner Time

Connect each animal to its food.

Robot

What is this robot's name?

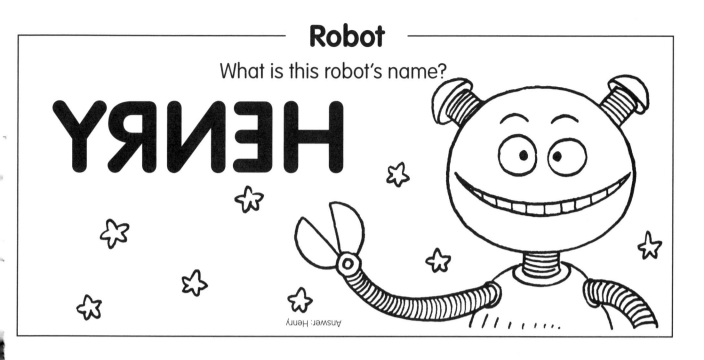

HENRY

Twig Game

Turn these six triangles into three triangles by removing only three twigs.

Vet

Connect the numbers to see which animal has a vet appointment.

Mixed-Up Story

Put these pictures in the correct order.

A

B

C

D

E

F

What Comes Next?

Finish each of these sequences. Draw the picture that comes next in each pattern.

1

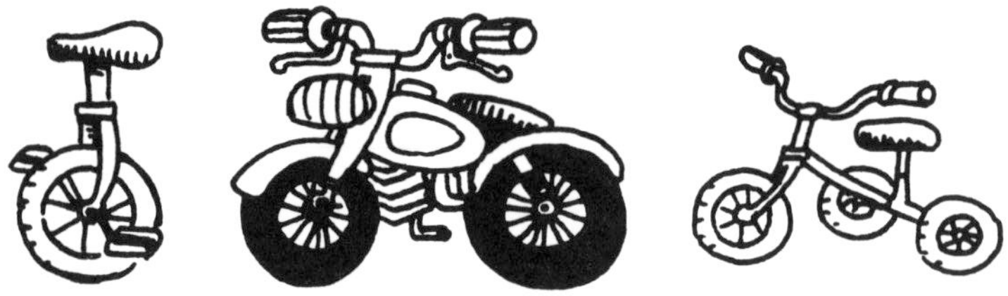

2   2   4   6   8

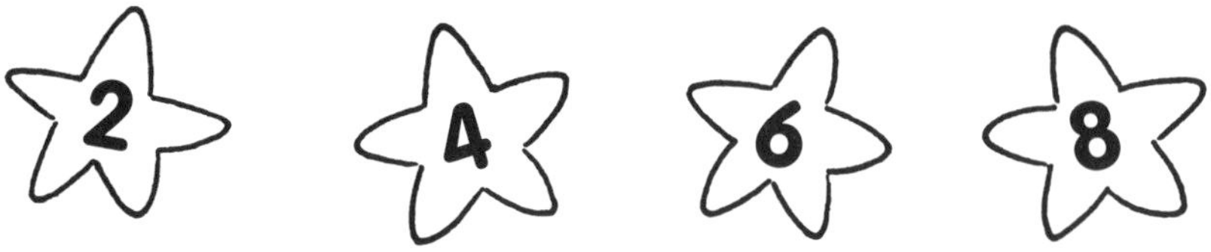

3

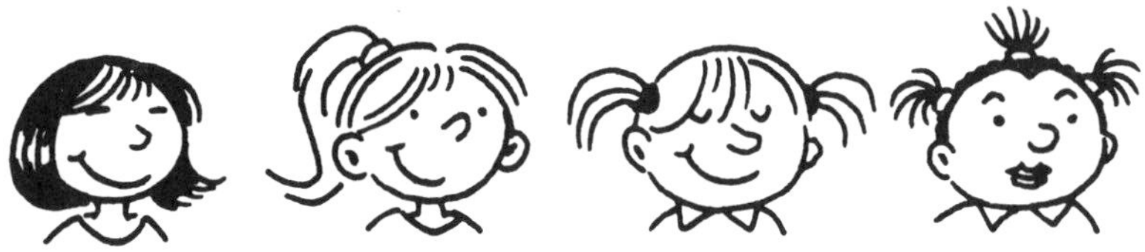

4

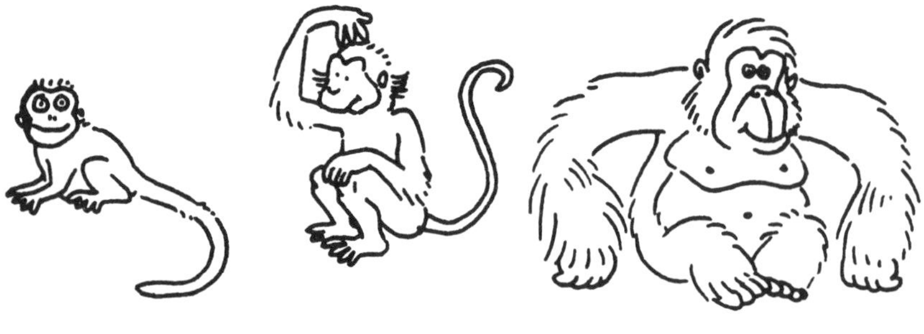

5   A   E   I   O

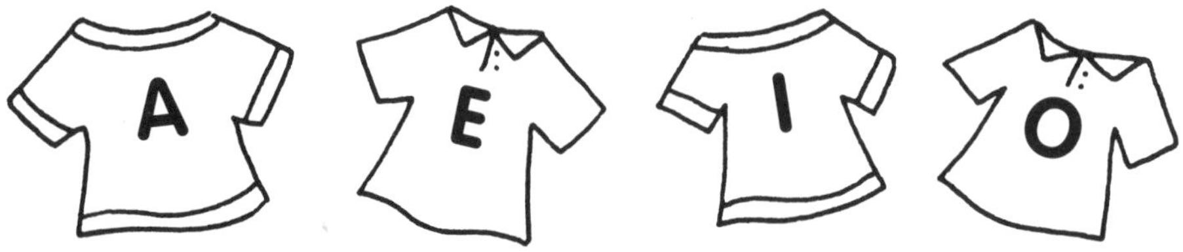

6

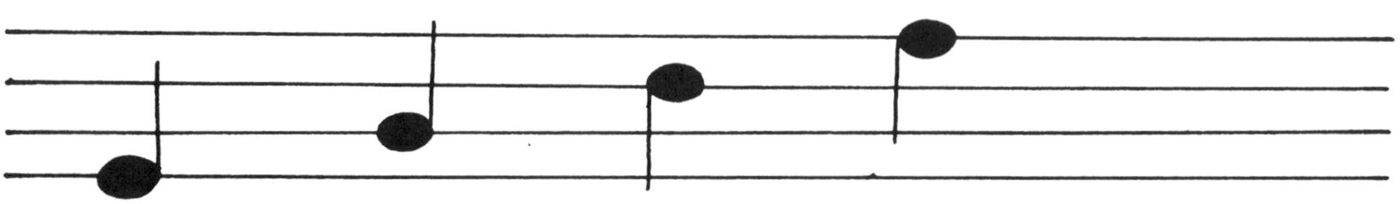

Snake Charmer

How tall is the snake? Add all the numbers up.

Riddle

How does a centipede walk over a dunghill?

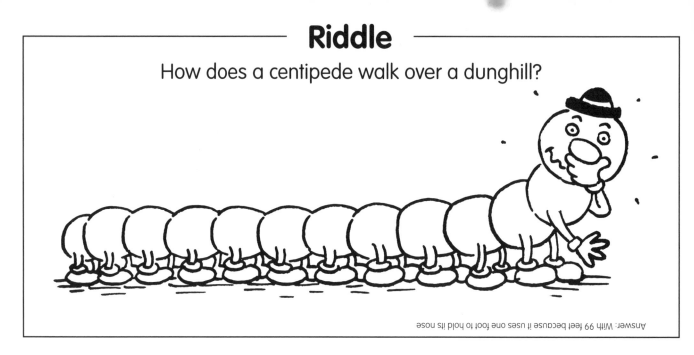

Answer: With 99 feet because it uses one foot to hold its nose

Tricky

Look closely at this shape. Is this an actual geometrical shape or is it an illusion?

Answer: an illusion

Shadow

Match the shadow to the correct kid.

Sandra　　　**Tom**　　　**Steven**

On Time

Draw the hands of each watch to match the time below it.

quarter after six　　　**8:45**　　　**10:20**

Magic Spell

What is the witch saying? Can you decipher her magic spell?

TRHSIQSZ
SNMZEKLOLPYZ SSOSUAP
RIOS
ADLEULIZCZINORUVSO!

Answer: Cross out every second letter and it will say: THIS SMELLY SOUP IS DELICIOUS

The Juggling Seal

Which professions can you read if you put the balls that Bobo is juggling in pairs?

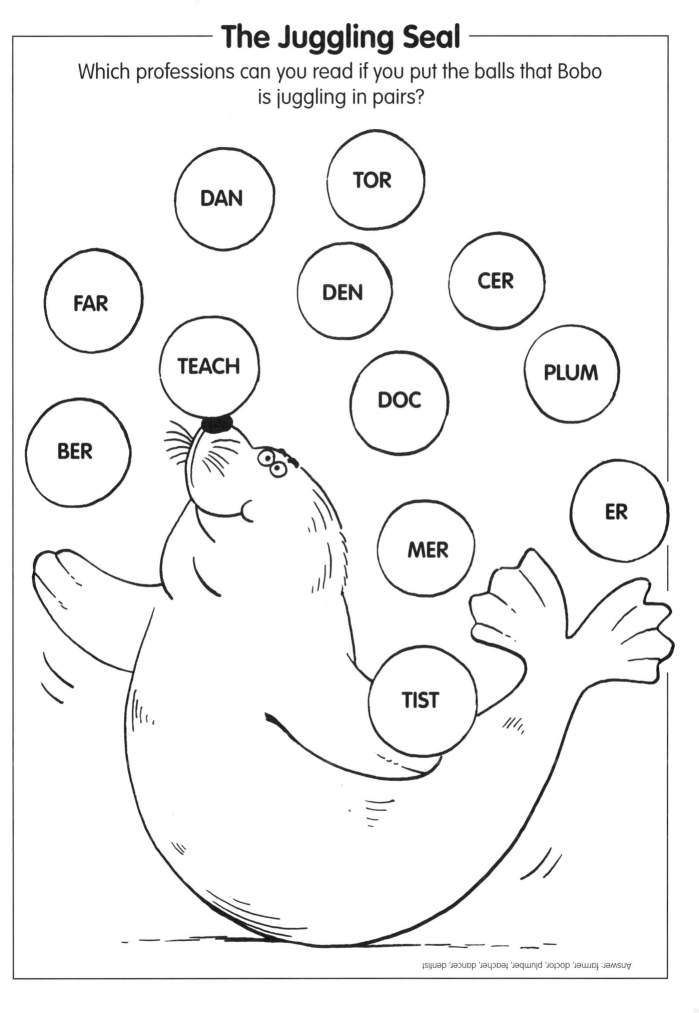

DAN

TOR

DEN

CER

FAR

TEACH

PLUM

DOC

BER

ER

MER

TIST

In the Museum

Color in all of the sections with a cross the same color.
What do you see in the painting?

Thief!

Find out which letters of the alphabet are missing in order to see what the thief is afraid of.

Drawing

Finish the picture by drawing the other half.

Careers

Connect each object with the appropriate person.

Paw Prints

Which of these paw prints is the grizzly bear's?

Pretty Dresses

Which of these dresses is identical to Lily's?

Billboard

The words have fallen off this billboard.
Can you put them back in order?

too! for

can

Meow!

The dogs

best cats! for Now

food

Crazy Clowns

Write the correct name next to each of these clowns. Pop is the tallest clown after Pip. Jolly is short, but not the shortest one. Flip is as tall as Flop, but not quite so fat. Colly is shorter than Flop.

1 ....

2 ....

3 ....

4 ....

5 ....

6 ....

Answer: 1 Pip, 2 Flip, 3 Pop, 4 Flop, 5 Colly, 6 Jolly

Menu

The menu has gotten all mixed up. Put the pieces in pairs and find out what dishes the guests have ordered.

SA

ONION

IPS

SPAG

APPLE

LAD

CH

ICE-

SOUP

PIE

CREAM

HETTI

Tractor

Which of these objects do you need to build a tractor?

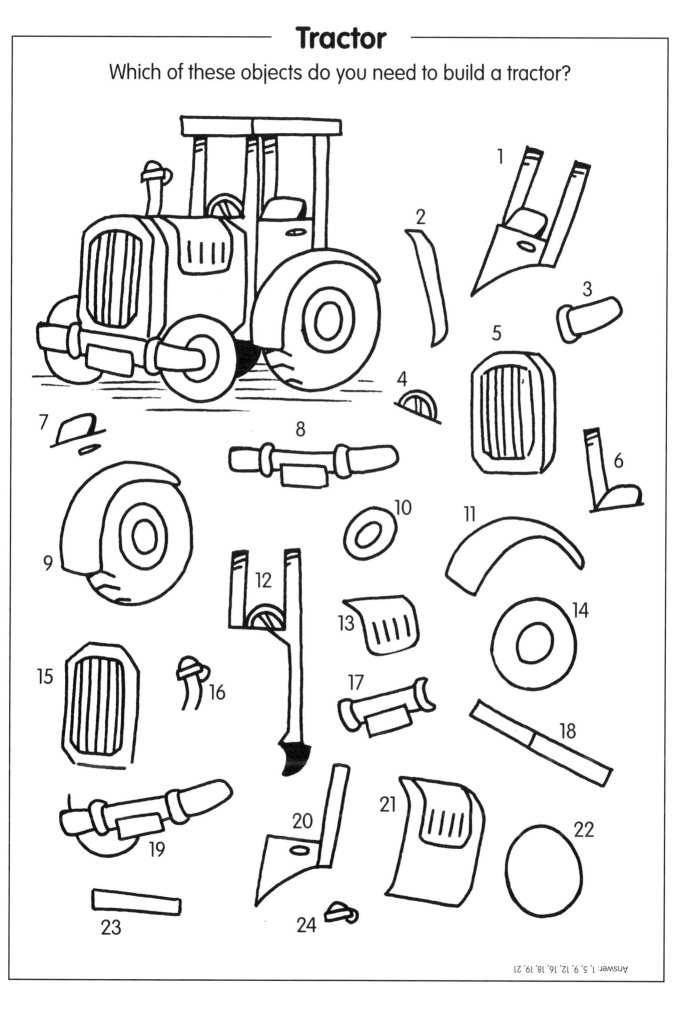

Count the Spots

How many spots does each of these snakes have?

Lisp

Slither

In the Garden

Circle the objects you need to work in the garden.

A Strange Animal

Which animals got mixed together here?

Trains

Fill in the missing numbers and add + or – where appropriate.

$$214 + \text{.......} = 346$$

$$16 \text{.......} 7 \text{.......} 4 = 13$$

$$30 + 5 + \text{.......} - 12 = 26$$

$$130 \text{.......} 12 + \text{.......} = 126$$

$$218 \text{.......} 105 \text{.......} 15 = 128$$

Seven Little Goats

The goats are hiding because the wolf is chasing them. Can you find all seven of them?

Space Journey

Where is the space shuttle flying off to? Connect all numbers that are multiples of 3, starting with 3 and going up to 36.

Twin Sisters

Two of these sisters are identical twins.
Can you find them?

Annie

Nanny

Lizzy

Jenny

Kitty

Lily

Puppy

Draw the picture of this puppy in the bottom grid.
Let the top grid help you with the shapes.

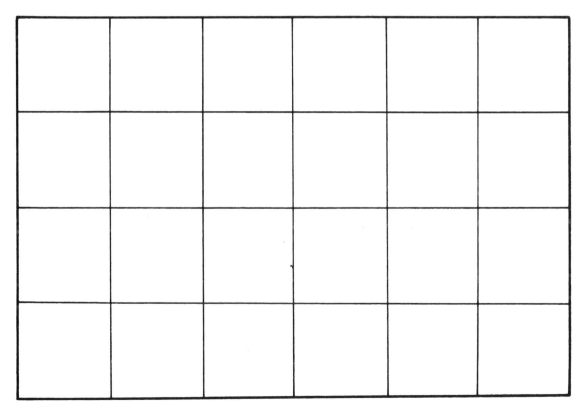

Puzzle

Which of these pieces matches the puzzle?

B.

A.

C.

Sports

Which sports are these children practicing?

Gnome

Which shadow belongs to the gnome?

1   2   3

Answer: 2

Creepy Maze

How can the little ghost find its way down through the maze of creepy faces?

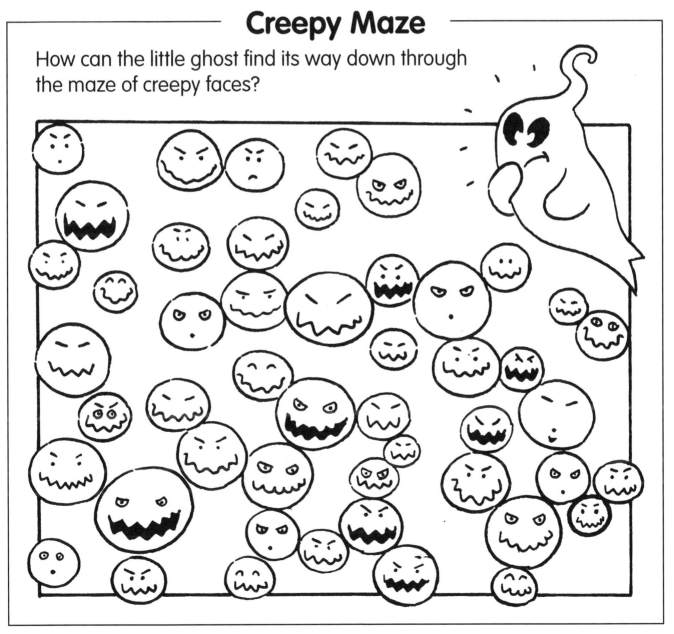

Waiter

What are the ten differences between the two pictures?

Marbles

Can you make pairs with all of the marbles? Afterwards, color the pairs the same. Be careful though—one marble doesn't make a pair!

Hidden Eggs

Henrietta the Hen has laid ten eggs, but she has hidden them and now cannot find them. Can you help find Henrietta's eggs?

Scary Path

Find the path to the castle. You can only walk horizontally and vertically.

You should follow the boxes in this order.

Build a Kite

Tim wants to build a kite. Draw a circle around
the objects that he needs.

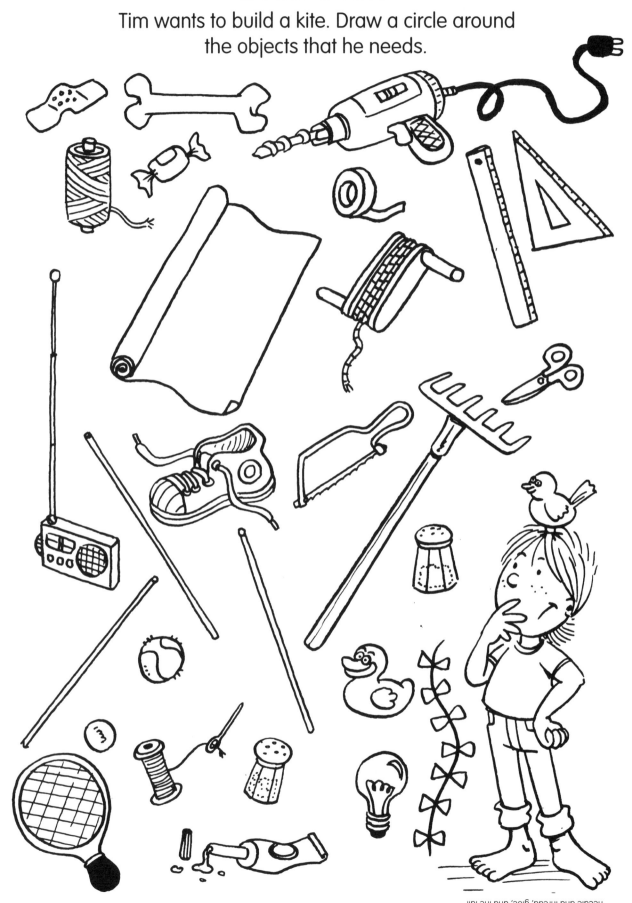

Shadow Play

Whose are these shadows?

Measuring

Which of the two vertical lines is the tallest one?

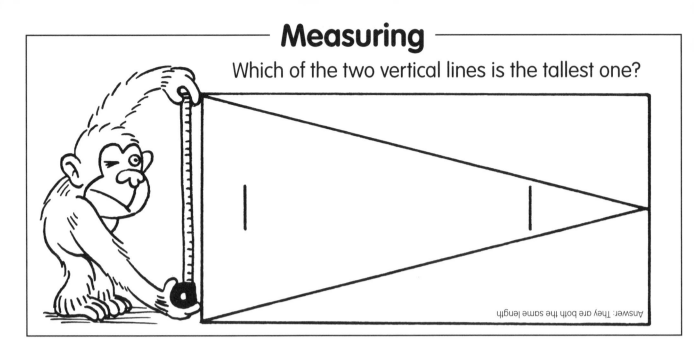

Answer: They are both the same length

Tumbling

How many tumbles did this little clown make?

Answer: 19

In the Sea

Do you know the names of these animals?

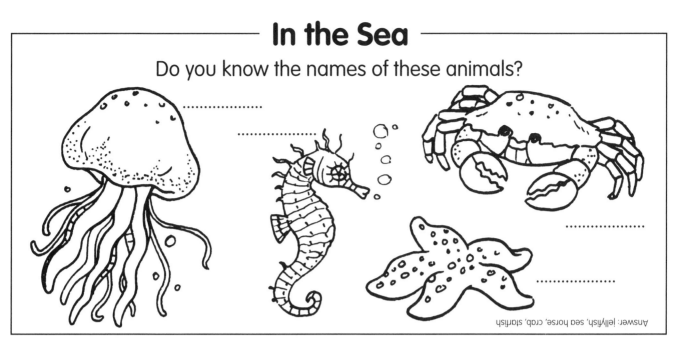

Staring at the stars

One of these stars is different from the others. Which one is it and why?

Robot Maze

How can our little robot reach the bottle of oil?

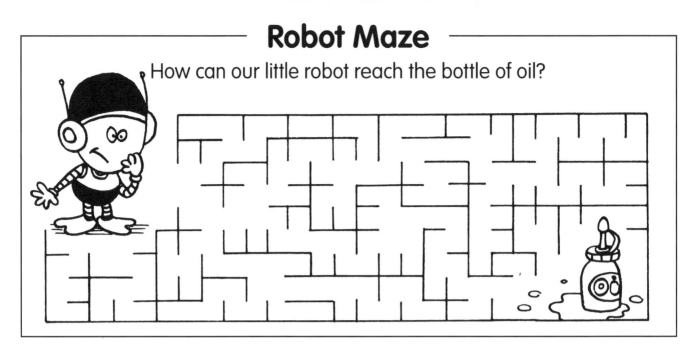

Diet

Piggy's doctor has put him on a healthy diet.
What is Piggy NOT allowed to eat?

Answer: cake, ice cream, chocolate bar, candy, potato chips

Beetles

Which of these beetles is heading straight to the sugar cube?

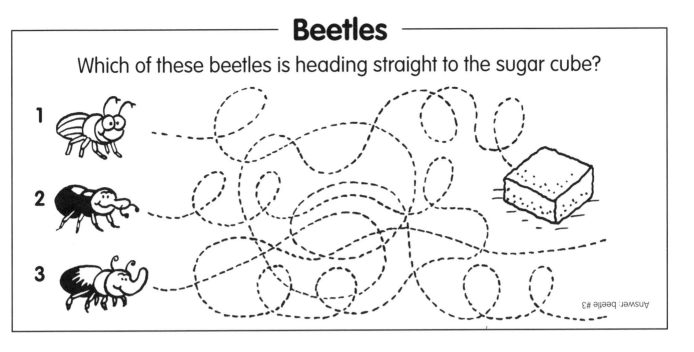

1

2

3

Spy X

Unmask the spy. Spy X has neither a beard nor moustache. Spy X doesn't wear a hat either. Spy X wears a long coat. Who is Spy X?

Jumping Rope

Which of the three images at the bottom of the page finishes the movement?

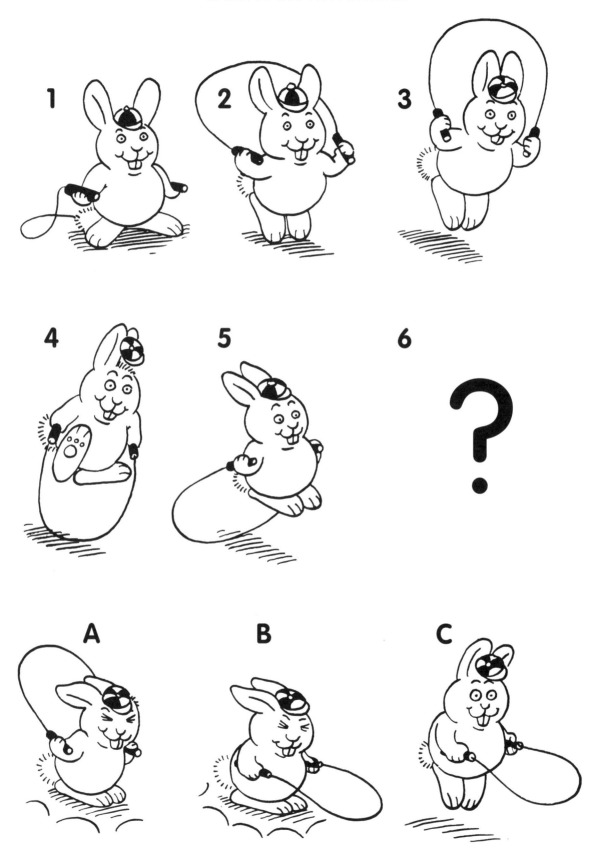

Find the Triangles

Can you find the 10 triangles that are hidden in this picture?

Tiles

Mr. Bear wants to tile this wall. Calculate how many tiles he will need for this job.

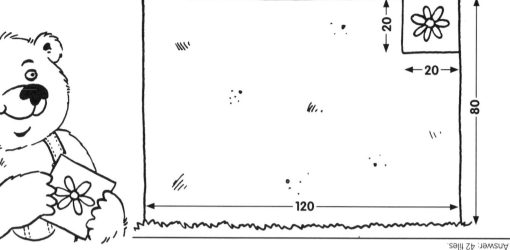

Extraterrestrial Sum

Help Bleep work out this sum. Find out what number each of the planets represents.

Tulips

Two of these tulips are identical. Color them red.

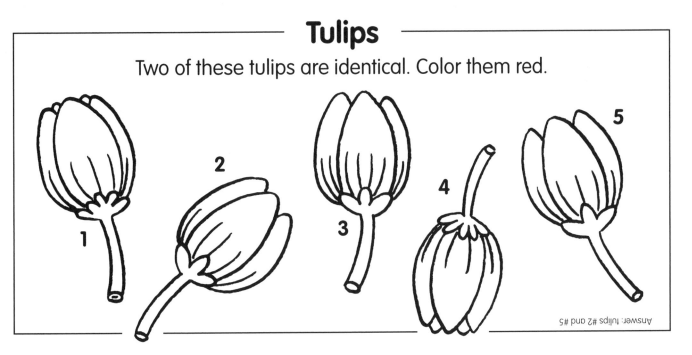

Building a Wall

How many building blocks does the mouse need to build a wall that is 40in. wide and 20in. tall? Each building block is 5in. high.

At the Beach

Little Lucy is going to the beach. What does she need to take with her?

Answer: sunglasses, umbrella, shovel, bucket, beach ball, suntan lotion.

Socks

Can you make pairs with these socks? Afterwards, color the pairs the same. Watch out though! One sock does not make a pair!

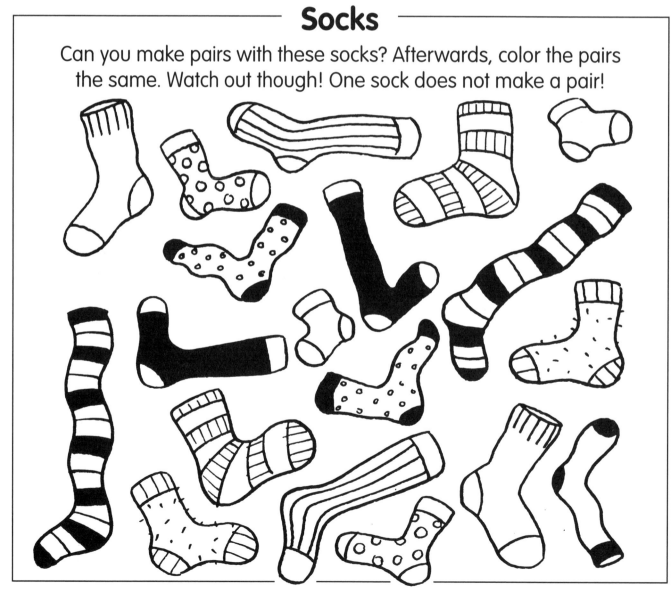

Starry Maze

Can you help Bleep find his way to his home planet?

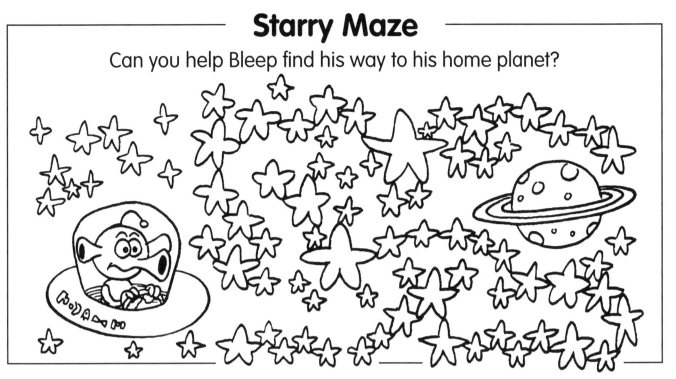

Jolly Jokers

These clowns have erased lots of letters on this board.
Can you still read what it says?

W.T.H

O.T F.R

S.LL.

.L.WN.!

Intruder

Which one of these animals doesn't live in the water?

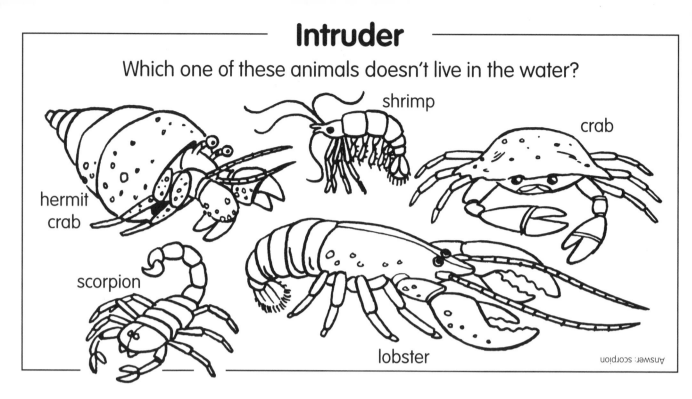

shrimp

crab

hermit crab

scorpion

lobster

Confusing Can

Piggy the cook doesn't remember what is in this can. He is quite sure that it is neither crab nor salmon, so you can cross out the letters of those words. What is in the can?

C T S
U R A
R N
N L A
O M B
A

Instruments

Which of these instruments doesn't belong here?

Answer: the violin because it is not an instrument you blow into.

Strange Bird?

What two things got mixed up in this picture? Think of a name for this strange bird and give it some funny colors.

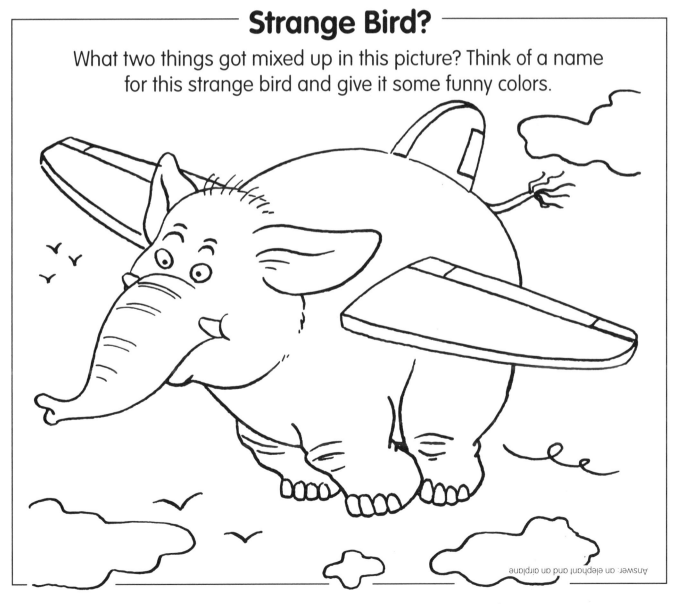

Answer: an elephant and an airplane

Build a Robot

Color the pieces that you will need to build this robot.

Catch a Butterfly!

Catch three butterflies whose numbers add up to 1000.

Three Bears in a Row

Place the squares at the bottom of this page so that there are always three bears in a row, vertically as well as horizontally.